T0114909

A THIRD OF THE SUBMARINES IN THE SEA DIED

WORMWOOD (CHERNOBYL)

JOHAN ANDREAS RAUTENBACH

WESTBOW
PRESS®
A DIVISION OF THOMAS NELSON
& ZONDERVAN

WestBow Press books may be ordered through booksellers or by contacting:

WestBow Press
A Division of Thomas Nelson & Zondervan
1663 Liberty Drive
Bloomington, IN 47403
www.westbowpress.com
844-714-3454

Scripture quotations are taken from the Holy Bible, King James Version.

ISBN: 979-8-3850-1458-3 (sc)
ISBN: 979-8-3850-1449-1 (e)

Library of Congress Control Number: 2023923754

Print information available on the last page.

WestBow Press rev. date: 12/15/2023

Contents

Introduction

Welcome to "The First Angel Sounded," a profound exploration of the collision between historical events and biblical prophecy, focusing on the lens of World War I. In these pages, we will navigate through the intricate web that links the echoes of the past with the revelations of scripture.

As the world descended into the chaos of the 20th century's first global conflict, little did anyone anticipate the far-reaching consequences that would reshape nations and forge new paths. This book uncovers how the aftermath of World War I not only transformed geopolitical landscapes but also intertwined with the words of ancient prophecies.

We will journey through the annals of history, tracing the roots of World War I and the threads that connected it with verses from sacred texts. By examining the historical events without embellishment and delving into the scriptural foresight, we aim to shed light on how seemingly unrelated elements can coalesce in a profound and unforeseen harmony.

"The First Angel Sounded" seeks to bridge the divide between the historical and the spiritual, offering readers an opportunity to reflect on the intricate interplay between human actions and divine revelations. By focusing on facts and context, we invite you to ponder the significance of how our world's course aligns with the wisdom and foresight found within ancient texts.

Through a straightforward exploration of the past and the timeless wisdom of scripture, this book aims to illuminate the interconnectedness between the events of history and the prophetic insights that have resonated across generations. Join us as we embark on a journey of discovery, seeking to understand the interwoven threads that bind human actions and the whispers of a higher design.

SECTION 1

THE FIRST ANGEL
SOUNDED: WWI

Revelation 8:7 reads, *"The first angel sounded, and there followed hail and fire mingled with blood, and they were cast upon the earth: and the third part of trees was burnt up, and all green grass was burnt up."*

Strongs 5464. Chalaza – χάλαζα = hailstone, hail.

Like a shotgun or hail gun. The artillery was loaded with shrapnel.

The interlinear bible says a third of the earth was burnt up. That does not mean the whole earth; it means a third of the war arena was burnt up.

The artillery of World War I, which led to trench warfare, was an important factor in the war. Revelation 8 portrays a moment of profound cosmic significance, as the first angel sounded its trumpet, unleashing a sequence of apocalyptic events upon the world. The initial blast brought forth a cataclysmic mix of hail and fire, resembling an ominous rain of blood. This haunting imagery evokes a sense of dread and turmoil, as nature itself seems to rebel against humanity. The hailstones, like celestial projectiles, fell with an unstoppable force, mirroring the destructive power of warfare.

Strongs 5464, "Chalaza," a term rooted in ancient language, paints a vivid picture of hailstones. Much like a barrage from a hail gun or a shotgun, these hailstones unleashed a barrage of devastation. Drawing a parallel, the artillery employed in warfare, particularly during World War I, comes to mind. Loaded with shrapnel, these artillery shells became instruments of widespread destruction, reshaping the battlefield and altering the dynamics of war.

The interlinear bible's assertion that a third of the earth was burnt up requires a nuanced interpretation. It's not a depiction of the entire planet ablaze, but rather a symbolic representation of a significant portion of the battleground being engulfed in flames. This imagery resonates with the tactics employed in trench warfare, a defining feature of World War I. This period saw artillery emerging as a game-changer, influencing military tactics, operations, and strategies. The fronts turned into mazes of trenches and barbed wire, where the balance of power seemed insurmountable.

The development of tanks and mortars in response to the trench warfare dilemma illustrates the desperate attempts to break the deadlock. Tanks were engineered to navigate the treacherous terrain of trenches, offering a glimmer of hope amidst the stagnant frontlines. Mortars, on the other hand, provided a means to rain down destruction from above, introducing a new vertical dimension to the conflicts that raged below.

To understand the magnitude of this transformation, one can look at the numbers of military field artillery by country in 1919. A visual representation of these figures reveals the staggering proliferation of artillery pieces, each a harbinger of destruction and upheaval. The relentless advancement of technology combined with the grim realities of warfare led to a reshaping of the battlefield's landscape, where the echoes of the trumpet from Revelation 8 seemed to reverberate in the chaos of World War I.

In this context, the trumpet's blast in Revelation 8 takes on a metaphorical significance. It heralds not only the cosmic events described but also symbolizes the relentless advance of human ingenuity and destruction, epitomized by the artillery of World War I. Just as the trumpet's call echoed through the ages, so too did the roar of cannons and the thunder of war reshape the world's destiny in the tumultuous years of the early 20th century.

Technology

The era of World War I, despite witnessing the emergence of groundbreaking technologies like aircraft, machine guns, and armoured vehicles, found its defining force in the form of artillery. The resounding echoes of cannon fire marked the heartbeats of battles, as artillery stood unwaveringly as the primary weapon throughout this period of global conflict. Amid the rapid advancements in weaponry, artillery's dominance remained unchallenged, casting a long shadow over the battlefield and shaping the course of the war. It's important to note that despite the arrival of modern innovations, the sheer destructive power and strategic versatility of artillery propelled it to the forefront of warfare.

Within the context of World War I, artillery held the mantle of being the paramount threat to ground troops. It's devastating impact reverberated across the battlefield, instilling fear and chaos among soldiers who found themselves at the mercy of the lethal artillery barrages. These barrages became synonymous with the brutal reality of trench warfare, a phenomenon that characterized the static and agonizingly prolonged nature of conflict during this era. The continuous bombardment of artillery shells transformed the landscape into a nightmarish terrain, where survival was an arduous struggle and advancement often seemed impossible.

Turning our gaze to the correlation between historical events and spiritual allegories, we find an intriguing connection between the trumpet blasts of Revelation and World War I. As we delve deeper into this discourse, it becomes evident that the first trumpet of Revelation bears uncanny resemblance to the cataclysmic events of WWI. This parallel becomes even more pronounced when we recognize that artillery occupied a central role in both narratives.

This synergy between Revelation and WWI becomes particularly apparent when we consider the description of artillery's effects as outlined in Revelation 8:7: "hail and fire mingled with blood." The haunting imagery conjured by this verse mirrors the harrowing reality of artillery warfare. It evokes the imagery of shrapnel rounds designed with the explicit purpose of inflicting harm upon infantry. The timed fuses, meticulously calibrated, triggered explosive havoc just above enemy formations, releasing a rain of metal balls that sliced through the air and flesh alike.

An evocative historical image from World War I captures the 14th Battery of Australian Field Artillery in action, loading a British 18-PDR field gun near Bellewaerde Lake in the Ypres Sector. This photograph encapsulates the gravity of the situation – colossal guns manned by determined soldiers, engaged in a fierce symphony of destruction. The artillery's roar serves as a grim reminder of the toll taken on both human lives and the landscapes that bore witness to their struggles.

The weaponry of World War I, reminiscent of oversized hail guns, held a singular purpose – to eradicate the lives of soldiers. The iron rain they produced symbolized not only physical destruction but also the transformation of battlefields into rivers of blood. The precise engineering that allowed these instruments of war to rain down death upon the enemy underlines the calculated cruelty of conflict. The bloodshed that ensued was a testament to the ruthless effectiveness of these artillery pieces, leaving an indelible mark on the annals of history.

In the complex tapestry of history and spirituality, the symbolism of Revelation's first trumpet finds resonance with the overwhelming power of artillery in World War I. The eerie congruence between the verses of ancient prophecy and the thunderous echoes of cannons underscores the idea that historical events, even those marked by human conflict, can evoke deeper spiritual contemplations. Just as artillery reshaped the physical landscape of war, the intersection of Revelation and history invites us to explore the multifaceted nature of our world and the narratives that shape it.

The 14th Battery of Australian Field Artillery, 5th Field Artillery Brigade, 2nd Division, loading a British 18-PDR field gun near Bellewaerde Lake, in the Ypres Sector. This is a picture from WW1 and in the Public Domain.

https://www.warhistoryonline.com/world-war-i/big-guns-the-devastating-field-artillery-of-ww1.html

High Explosives and Propellants

The annals of the First World War bear witness to an unprecedented scale of artillery engagement, marked by the deployment of an astronomical quantity of artillery shells laden with high explosives. This deployment, a hallmark of modern warfare, underscores the profound impact of technological advancement on the nature of conflict during this era.

A stark illustration of this artillery's prevalence emerges from the empirical data. British 18-pounder guns, renowned for their potency, discharged an astounding 86 million shells throughout the course of the war. The magnitude of this figure underscores the sheer volume of ordinance directed toward the theater of battle. Similarly, the German offensive launched upon the city of Verdun on 21 February 1916 initiated with a bombardment involving 100,000 shells in the initial hour. This numerical intensity serves as a testament to the calculated use of high explosives as a strategic tool.

The defining attribute of these high explosives is their capacity for instantaneous detonation, with shock waves propagating at speeds surpassing that of sound itself. The arsenal of war encompassed a diverse range of explosive compounds. Among them, picric acid, characterized by the chemical formula $C_6H_2(NO_2)_3OH$ and the IUPAC name 2,4,6-trinitrophenol, achieved notoriety. Noteworthy is the British designation "lyddite," named after Lydd, a town in southern England where production was centered.

Trinitrotoluene (TNT), denoted by the formula C6H2(NO2)3CH3, assumed prominence as a high explosive universally embraced by all sides in the conflict. This compound, whose origins trace back to the meticulous efforts of a German chemist in 1863, emerged as a quintessential element in artillery ordnance.

Further complicating the landscape of explosives was ammonal, a composite amalgamation of ammonium nitrate (NH4NO3) and aluminum. Its application extended beyond shell fillings to encompass hand grenades, trench mortar bombs, and underground tunnelling operations. This versatility encapsulated the multifaceted role of such compounds in the wartime context.

A critical facet of warfare is its reliance on resource availability. The dwindling supply of TNT during the conflict prompted the British to devise an alternative, known as amatol. This amalgam, blending TNT and ammonium nitrate, was a response to the exigencies of war, illustrating the pragmatic adaptations necessitated by resource limitations.

The saga of World War I becomes indelibly intertwined with the symphony of artillery, a manifestation of the fusion between technological innovation and the mechanics of destruction. The monumental deployment of high explosives underscores the dualities of human capability: the capacity for innovation that advances societies, juxtaposed against the potential for devastation that conflict reveals.

and the third part of trees was burnt up, and all green grass was burnt up.

Now we can start looking at the pictures of the battlefields. Start by looking at the picture of Messines Ridge. See what the trees and grass look like.

German trench destroyed by a mine explosion, 1917. About 10,000 German troops were killed when the 19 mines were detonated. This is a photo of WW1 and in the Public Domain.

https://en.wikipedia.org/wiki/Battle_of_Messines_(1917)

Battle of the Somme

More than three million men fought in the battle and one million men were wounded or killed, making it one of the deadliest battles in human history.

The Battle of the Somme was one of the costliest battles of World War I. The original Allied estimate of casualties on the Somme, made at the Chantilly Conference on 15 November 1916, was that the Germans suffered 630,000 casualties, exceeding the 485,000 suffered by the British and French. As one German officer wrote,

"Somme. The whole history of the world cannot contain a ghastlier word."

—Friedrich Steinbrecher

Soldiers digging a communication trench through Delville Wood. This is a photo of WW1 and in the Public Domain.

https://en.wikipedia.org/wiki/Battle_of_the_Somme

During the Battle of Morval on September 25, 1916, an intriguing symbolism emerges beyond the battlefield. The visual of British troops advancing carries a hidden meaning through the imagery of grass and trees.

In this context, trees symbolize important individuals with influence, akin to towering figures in history. Grass, on the other hand, represents ordinary people forming the foundation of society.

This symbolism underscores the complex dynamics between leaders and the masses. It's a reminder of how influential individuals shape history, while everyday people sustain societies. The battle's imagery prompts us to reflect on the profound forces that mold civilizations, connecting history, spirituality, and symbolism in subtle ways.

World War I Casualties

The toll exacted by World War I on both military personnel and civilians remains staggering, with a cumulative casualty count of approximately 40 million. These casualties encompass a broad spectrum, including an estimated 15 to 22 million deaths and around 23 million wounded military individuals. This war has etched its place in history as one of the most lethal conflicts humanity has witnessed.

This overall death count incorporates 9 to 11 million military personnel, while the civilian toll stands at 6 to 13 million. Within the framework of the conflict, the Triple Entente, also recognized as the Allies, endured losses of about 6 million military personnel, while the Central Powers suffered approximately 4 million casualties. An additional 2 million lives succumbed to diseases, and a haunting 6 million were classified as missing, presumed deceased. These grim statistics are grounded in authoritative published sources, forming a stark testament to the realities of war.

Contrasting the military fatalities in World War I with earlier 19th-century conflicts, it's notable that approximately two-thirds of military deaths occurred in direct combat scenarios. This stands in contrast to earlier conflicts where the majority of casualties resulted from disease. Nonetheless, the specter of disease, including the profound impact of the 1918 flu pandemic, as well as deaths occurring among prisoners of war, contributed to roughly a third of total military fatalities across all involved parties.

The recorded casualties of World War I are an indelible marker of the human cost of conflict, prompting somber reflection on the repercussions of global turmoil. This grim historical record underscores the profound societal shifts that emerged from this catastrophic event, shaping the course of nations and humanity itself.

Is this the third of the "and the third part of trees was burnt up"?

Let's see what the Bible has to say about trees and grass.

Trees

Throughout the Bible, the use of trees as symbols carries profound meaning, offering insights into the dynamics of kingdoms and rulers. In the book of Daniel (4:24-26), the towering tree serves as an allegory for Nebuchadnezzar, the formidable king of Babylon. This imagery highlights the fleeting nature of power and the divine orchestration that governs rulers and empires. Similarly, the image of expansive branches finds resonance in the depiction of Pharaoh and his kingdom, showcasing a divine proclamation through the words of the Lord God.

These symbolic portrayals are not isolated instances. Consider the narrative in Judges (9:14-15), where Abimelech's pursuit of kingship takes center stage. Through a parable of trees, the story reflects on the implications of seeking authority and dominance. This theme reverberates across history, echoing the patterns of ambition and the consequences of straying from intended paths.

The allegorical significance of trees continues into the New Testament, as seen in Romans (11:15-17). Here, the apostle employs the metaphor of an olive tree to illustrate Israel's place within the divine plan. The connection between holiness and lineage underscores the spiritual threads that bind generations and nations together. This symbolic resonance echoes in the verses of Revelation (11:4), where two olive trees and candlesticks represent the collective witness of Israel and the church, illuminating the spiritual landscape with their presence.

Within the context of Revelation's imagery, the burning of a third of the trees finds deeper resonance when viewed as the burning of kingdoms. Trees, in this symbolic framework, represent realms of governance and authority. Applying this interpretation to World War I, the imagery may point to the devastation experienced by certain nations, notably Germany, which bore the brunt of conflict's impact.

The recurring motif of trees as carriers of symbolic significance underscores the layers of wisdom concealed within biblical narratives. These allegorical elements serve as enduring lessons, applicable across time and circumstance. They guide our understanding of power dynamics, ambition, and the divine hand that shapes the destinies of individuals, nations, and humanity as a whole. In this symbology, the whispers of history and spirituality intermingle, inviting contemplation and introspection.

All the grass was burnt up Revelation 8:7:

"The first angel sounded, and there followed hail and fire mingled with blood, and they were cast upon the earth: and the third part of trees was burnt up, and all green grass was burnt up."

The profound symbolism woven into biblical narratives often transcends the surface meaning of words, offering layers of interpretation that resonate through time. In Revelation's vivid imagery of "all the green grass was burnt up," a multi-faceted allegory emerges. It is not merely a representation of the physical landscape ravaged by fire, but a poignant reflection of the emotional landscape of those who endured the tumult of World War I. As the battlefields blazed, they bore witness to the withering of life, much like the grass consumed by flames. But this imagery also serves as a mirror to the souls of the soldiers, scarred by the horrors they experienced.

The term "post-traumatic stress disorder" (PTSD) may be a modern label, but its essence reverberates throughout history. The war's toll on mental well-being is undeniable. The trenches, once a sanctuary for survival, evolved into harbingers of trauma. Witnessing the agonies of war, whether it be the constant artillery bombardment or the grisly conditions in the trenches, left an indelible mark on those who fought. The echoes of gunfire still resonate in the minds of survivors, long after the last shot was fired. This psychological aftermath becomes a testament to the enduring impact of conflict, a testament that connects the past to the present.

Prophecy Unveiled: Israel and Jerusalem as Key Players

In the grand tapestry of biblical prophecy, the figures of Israel and Jerusalem stand as focal points. They serve as the bedrock upon which prophetic events unfold, consistently anchoring the narratives. In the context of World War I, the pivotal role of Israel within prophecies gains new dimensions. The historical events of the war align strikingly with the symbolism depicted in Revelation, solidifying the connection between the spiritual and material realms.

The Balfour Declaration, a seminal moment in history, reverberates as a pointer to prophetic fulfillment. Issued on November 2, 1917, it set forth the recognition of a homeland for the Jewish people in Palestine. This historic declaration resonates deeply with biblical narratives, echoing the importance of Jerusalem and Israel in the divine scheme. Furthermore, the capture of Jerusalem by an entity embodying Israel, specifically Great Britain, marks a significant turning point. The surrender of Jerusalem on December 9, 1917, holds profound spiritual significance as well. This date, 24 Kislev 5678, serves as a nexus, bridging the tangible events of history with spiritual realities, underscoring that the movements of nations are intertwined with the unfolding of divine plans.

The web of confirmations extends beyond the echoes of history. Half a century later, the recapture of Jerusalem in 1967 during the six-day war reaffirms its spiritual centrality. This event becomes a living testament to the city's enduring significance in prophetic narratives. A century later, in 2017, Donald Trump's declaration recognizing Jerusalem as Israel's capital and moving the U.S. embassy stands as another chapter in this intricate narrative. The United States, representing the collective tribes of Israel, echoes the symbolism of unity. This symbolism transcends the material realm, reflecting the spiritual unity of a dispersed people.

In Matthew 24:6-8, Jesus' words resound with a timeless resonance. The "beginning of sorrows" encompasses not only the Great War but also the sequence of events that reverberate across time. World War I emerges as the first trumpet, setting in motion a sequence that aligns with prophetic intervals. The war becomes the harbinger of tribulations, echoing its toll in the subsequent famines and pestilences that humanity faced. The interplay of these elements reveals a somber truth—that conflict's ripples extend far beyond the battlefield, manifesting in the realms of hunger, disease, and societal upheaval.

In this intricate nexus of symbolism, history, and prophecy, we find a reminder of the complexities of existence. The narratives of grass and trees intertwine with the struggles of soldiers and the destinies of nations. The echoes of trauma and triumph, inscribed in history's annals, compel us to reflect on the fragility of human endeavor and the enduring strength of spiritual undercurrents. This rich tapestry, woven through the pages of scripture and the annals of time, invites us to traverse the corridors of meaning, delving deeper into the interconnected narratives that shape our world. As we contemplate the multifaceted dimensions of these events, we discover a profound interplay between human choices and divine orchestration, a dance that continues to unfold across the chapters of history.

Unveiling the Hidden Toll: Famine and Disease in the Wake of World War I

The impact of World War I reached far beyond the battlefield, leaving an indelible mark on humanity's history. While the conventional understanding of war often conjures images of gas attacks, artillery fire, and tanks, there existed another weapon—a silent adversary that waged its campaign far from the frontlines. This weapon was hunger, and it wielded its devastating power across the world long after the guns fell silent on November 11, 1918.

The Persian Famine of 1917-1919

The Persian Famine of 1917-1919 stands as a poignant testament to the far-reaching consequences of war. Within this three-year period, an estimated 2 million lives succumbed to hunger and diseases, including cholera, plague, and typhus. The grip of the famine was further tightened by the influenza outbreak that spread like wildfire, exacerbated by the concurrent 1918 flu pandemic. The toll it exacted was not confined to mere numbers; it revealed the insidious aftermath of conflict, where the effects of war rippled through communities, claiming lives even after the guns fell silent.

The Great Famine of Mount Lebanon

Another chapter of this somber narrative unfolds with the Great Famine of Mount Lebanon, spanning the years 1915 to 1918. During this period, a staggering 200,000 individuals, primarily Christian and Druze inhabitants, fell victim to mass starvation. Amidst the turmoil of World War I, the famine cast its shadow, amplifying the suffering of those caught in the crossfire of conflict. It serves as a stark reminder that the tendrils of war reach deep into the fabric of societies, impacting lives in ways that extend beyond the scope of battles and geopolitics.

The Iranian Holocaust: Unveiling a Concealed Tragedy

Among the most devastating chapters of this post-war narrative is the Iranian Holocaust. From 1917 to 1919, a period synonymous with turmoil, approximately 8 to 10 million Iranians perished due to starvation and disease. This catastrophe, concealed for nearly a century, emerges as one of the worst genocides of the 20th century. Within the broader context of World War I, this humanitarian crisis stands as a grim reminder of the interconnectedness of global events, revealing the profound human cost of conflict.

Hunger's Lingering Echoes: The Aftermath of World War I

While World War I formally concluded in 1918, the impact of conflict extended far beyond that watershed moment. The Hunger Draws the Map project, spearheaded by historians Dr. Mary Cox and Dr. Clare Morelon in collaboration with Professor Sir Hew Strachan, delves into the aftermath of the war, revealing how the Great War shaped the trajectory of nations through a lens often overlooked—food scarcity. The British and French blockade, aimed at hindering the flow of supplies to certain nations until 1919, left a trail of malnutrition and starvation across Europe and the Ottoman Empire.

The project underscores how fundamental needs—such as sustenance—played a pivotal role in shaping the course of post-war nations. The world witnessed how the absence of provisions reverberated long after the guns ceased firing. As we delve into this exploration, it becomes evident that history's tapestry is woven with intricate threads, where the resonance of hunger's impact is a testament to the profound and enduring influence of World War I. Beyond the chronicles of battles, this exploration of hunger serves as a testament to the broader, lasting consequences of war on the human experience.

Hunger

Beyond the epic battles and grand strategies that define history's narratives, there lies a darker aspect—the use of hunger as a weapon. In the annals of warfare, the role of hunger is often overshadowed, but its significance cannot be underestimated. A case in point is the British utilization of hunger as a tool to subdue the enemy during the tumultuous times leading up to World War I.

The Anglo-Boer War:
Hunger as a Silent Weapon

The Anglo-Boer War, often likened to Britain's Vietnam or Afghanistan, casts a revealing light on the tactics employed in conflict. Amidst this war's tumultuous landscape, hunger emerged as a formidable weapon. The British aimed to demoralize the Boers, using tactics that would echo through history. Concentration camps, a term that has become chillingly synonymous with suffering and loss, were established. Their purpose was to strike at the heart of Boer resistance by targeting women and children. However, what was meant to demoralize had an unforeseen effect—instead of breaking the Boers, it strengthened their resolve.

Calculations Gone Awry: The Boer War's Impact

The Boer War stands as a stark example of gross miscalculations, both militarily and politically, on the part of British leadership. With the aim to subdue the Boers, Britain employed an array of resources—more troops, greater expenditures, and a staggering loss of soldiers. This expenditure of human lives and resources marked a striking contrast between the Napoleonic Wars and World War I, an era in which Britain was fervently expanding its empire.

Echoes of Tragedy: Concentration Camps and South African Deaths

The specter of history's past is not easily forgotten. More than a century after the events that transpired in the South African War between 1899 and 1902, the legacy of that era reverberates. Over 48,000 lives were claimed in concentration camps, a grim testament to the dire consequences of utilizing hunger as a weapon. This chapter in history, often referred to as the Anglo-Boer War, casts a long shadow, reminding us of the multifaceted impact of conflict.

Reflections on Warfare and Humanity

As we examine history's pages, the role of hunger as a tool of war underscores the complexities of conflict. It offers a somber reminder that beyond the clashes of armies and the grand strategies of nations, there exists a human toll that reverberates for generations. The echoes of the past continue to resound in today's headlines, a stark reminder that history's scars are not easily erased. Amidst the tragedies, there's an opportunity for reflection on the methods employed in warfare. Hunger, once a silent weapon, emerges as a poignant reminder that the cost of conflict transcends boundaries and eras, underscoring the profound impact on human lives and shaping the course of history in ways often unforeseen.

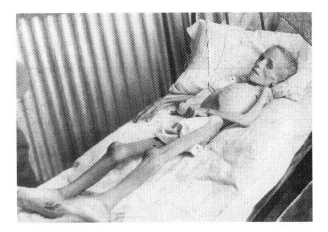

Lizzie van Zyl, a Boer child, visited by Emily Hobhouse in a British concentration camp. This is a photo of the Anglo Boer war around 1899 to 1902.

https://en.wikipedia.org/wiki/Second_Boer_War#/media/ File:LizzieVanZyl.jpg

This work is in the public domain in its country of origin and other countries and areas where the copyright term is the author's life plus 70 years or more.

Pestilences

The pages of history bear witness to events that echo through time, leaving an indelible imprint on human memory. The Spanish flu pandemic, also known as the Great Influenza epidemic or the 1918 influenza pandemic, emerges as a stark reminder of humanity's vulnerability in the face of microscopic adversaries. Caused by the H1N1 influenza A virus, this pandemic stands as a haunting chapter that transcended borders and redefined the fabric of societies.

Origins of Desolation: The Spanish Flu's Unassuming Beginnings

The genesis of the Spanish flu pandemic can be traced back to a seemingly unremarkable incident in March 1918, when the first documented case emerged in Kansas, United States. Swiftly, the virus journeyed across continents, casting its sinister shadow over France, Germany, and the United Kingdom in April. This microscopic entity swiftly evolved into a global catastrophe, revealing the fragile interconnectivity of our world.

Waves of Affliction:
The Unrelenting Onslaught

The Spanish flu pandemic unfurled in four successive waves, akin to relentless tides of affliction. This orchestrated symphony of devastation tested the resilience of societies and challenged the capacities of healthcare systems. Within a mere two years, approximately one-third of the global population—roughly 500 million individuals—succumbed to its grasp, leaving communities shattered and lives altered irreversibly.

A Grim Accounting: The Tragic Toll

Behind the numbers and statistics lie individual stories of heartache and loss. The Spanish flu pandemic's death toll is estimated to range from 17 million to a staggering 100 million lives—a testament to the unpredictability of such virulent outbreaks. This mortality toll serves as a haunting reminder of the pandemic's indiscriminate reach, transcending borders, ages, and social strata.

A Glimpse into Prophecy:
Spanish Flu and Its Context

The convergence of historical events and prophetic utterances is illuminated by the emergence of the Spanish flu pandemic. Its timing, coinciding with the biblical assertion of "All these are the beginning of sorrows," offers a profound connection between faith and history. This synchronicity invites contemplation on the interplay between celestial narratives and the human journey, sparking reflections on the cosmic design that shapes our existence.

World War I, a crucible of innovation and ingenuity, thrust humanity into an era of unprecedented warfare marked by the emergence of groundbreaking war machines. Amid the tumult of the battlefield, the stage was set for the debut of three revolutionary instruments—the submarine, the tank, and the airplane. These marvels of engineering and strategy would forever reshape the contours of war and evoke intriguing parallels with ancient texts.

Submarines:
Silent Intruders of the Deep

The confluence of technological prowess and historical context gave birth to submarines—a new dimension of warfare beneath the waves. As World War I unfolded, submarines emerged from the depths, demonstrating their capacity to rewrite naval strategy. These undersea vessels played a dual role—initially targeting warships, then redirecting their efforts towards merchant shipping. The impact was profound, sparking diplomatic tensions and entangling neutral nations in a web of unrest.

Interestingly, these aquatic marvels find resonance in ancient scripts that allude to vessels of the sea, evoking a sense of continuity between history's pages and the boundless ocean of prophecy.

Tanks: Breakthrough in Trench Warfare

The desolation of trench warfare on the Western Front cast a shadow over World War I. The impasse demanded a novel solution, and tanks emerged as a beacon of innovation. They traversed the quagmire of the battlefield, armored fortresses that defied the stalemate. These mechanical giants were not only a response to trench warfare but also a realization of long-envisioned concepts of armored mobility.

Curiously, references to fortified chariots and impenetrable shields in ancient writings eerily mirror the birth of tanks on the battlefield. The juxtaposition of scripture and reality invites contemplation on the intricate choreography of history.

Aircraft: Wings of Warfare

Above the fray of trenches and beneath the waves of the sea, the skies became a canvas for aerial prowess. Airplanes soared into the annals of warfare, introducing reconnaissance, dogfights, and strategic bombing. This aerial dimension became a new arena of conflict, propelling human imagination to unforeseen heights.

Oddly reminiscent of ancient metaphorical depictions of celestial beings and winged entities, airplanes symbolize the fusion of prophecy and reality—a realization of visions that transcend epochs.

The Confluence of Prophetic Threads and Historical Progress

The intersection of innovation and ancient prophecy weaves a captivating tapestry in the annals of history. As submarines, tanks, and airplanes debuted during World War I, one cannot help but discern the echoes of scripture, suggesting a harmonious convergence between human ingenuity and celestial narratives.

These war machines not only redefined warfare but also echoed long-standing visions. The seamless merging of historical events and prophetic allegory underlines the symphony that resonates across the ages—a symphony that beckons us to explore the interplay between destiny and human endeavor.

In the crucible of war, where human invention melds with the threads of fate, a tapestry of narratives emerges, inviting us to fathom the delicate balance between prophecy and progress. As history unfolds, the legacy of these war machines continues to illuminate the enigmatic dance between divination and human agency.

Battle of Cambrai (1917)

The Battle of Cambrai, alternatively known as the First Battle of Cambrai and Schlacht von Cambrai, marked a significant juncture within the First World War's tumultuous landscape. It witnessed a British offensive followed by the most substantial German counter-attack against the British Expeditionary Force (BEF) since 1914.

Taking place on the historic grounds of Cambrai, this battle etched its mark in the annals of history as a pivotal engagement that reshaped the course of the war. It exemplified the shifting dynamics of warfare, introducing new strategies and tactics that would leave an indelible impact on subsequent conflicts.

The battle's historical importance is underscored by its role in driving technological innovation. The use of mechanized warfare, including the introduction of tanks, marked a departure from traditional methods and heralded a new era of combat tactics. This transition demonstrated the adaptability and evolution of warfare in response to the changing landscape of the battlefield.

The Battle of Cambrai was more than a clash of forces; it was a manifestation of the ever-changing nature of warfare. The ebb and flow of the battle highlighted the fluidity and unpredictability that characterized the conflict. It showcased the resilience and determination of both sides, as well as their capacity to adapt to emerging challenges.

The significance of this battle extends beyond its historical context. It serves as a symbolic representation of the larger themes present in World War I—the interplay between innovation and tradition, the pursuit of strategic advantage, and the human cost of conflict. The events that unfolded at Cambrai underscore the complexities of war and the profound impact it has on societies and nations.

The Battle of Cambrai's legacy reverberates through time, resonating as a testament to the relentless march of history and the profound lessons it imparts. It stands as a reminder of the sacrifices made and the evolution of warfare that continues to shape the world. As we reflect on this battle, we are reminded of the enduring impact of human endeavors and the intricate interplay of history's threads.

As a forerunner of prophesy in the bible let us have a preview of a modern tank.

Battle of Megiddo (1918)

The pages of history unfold to reveal the resounding echoes of the Battle of Megiddo, a watershed moment that encapsulated the complex interplay of strategic maneuvering and historical resonance. Spanning from September 19 to September 25 in the year 1918, this battle etched its significance on the Plain of Sharon, unfurling its drama in front of notable locales such as Tulkarm, Tabsor, and Arara in the Judean Hills, as well as on the expansive Esdralon Plain, which bore witness to the epic struggles of Nazareth, Afulah, Beisan, Jenin, and Samakh.

Known by various names, including Megiddo Muharebesi in Turkish, the Nablus Hezimeti ("Rout of Nablus"), and the Nablus Yarması ("Breakthrough at Nablus"), the nomenclature chosen by General Allenby held a deep resonance, both biblical and symbolic in nature. However, it is worth noting that the nomenclature's fidelity to the specifics of the battle itself has been scrutinized, with some asserting that the connection might be somewhat misleading due to the limited fighting near Tel Megiddo itself.

The overarching significance of the Battle of Megiddo finds its nexus in the pivotal figure of General Allenby, a commander whose actions carried far-reaching implications that extended beyond the realm of warfare. General Allenby's indelible mark was not solely confined to the military sphere; his journey bore profound prophetic significance.

The year 1917 saw General Allenby's triumphant entry into Jerusalem as the representative of the British forces. This momentous event bore monumental prophetic undertones, intertwined with the historical and spiritual tapestry that encompassed the city's rich heritage. The prophetic connotations of this event, embedded in the very essence of Jerusalem, reverberated with profound implications that rippled through history.

It is within this intricate context that General Allenby, a harbinger of transformative change, unveils another layer of prophetic significance through his actions. The Battle of Megiddo, a canvas painted with the hues of conflict and strategy, served as the herald of greater events—the clarion call signaling the inception of the trumpets, a precursor to the cataclysmic seventh trumpet, often associated with the Battle of Armageddon. The confluence of history, strategy, and prophetic symbolism converged to create a narrative imbued with deeper meanings.

The Battle of Megiddo, therefore, emerges as a canvas where strategic intricacies and historical resonance intertwine. The maneuvers and clashes on these historic grounds encompassed more than the exchange of fire; they encapsulated the interplay of human agency and the broader currents of history. The implications of the battle ripple through time, inviting contemplation on the intricate dance between individual actions and the grand sweep of historical forces.

As we delve into the annals of history, the Battle of Megiddo beckons us to decipher its multi-layered significance—a convergence of military strategy, symbolic resonance, and the underlying current of prophecy. It embodies the enigmatic relationship between the past, present, and future, reminding us that history's pages are often illuminated by moments that transcend the confines of their time and space. In the echoes of Megiddo, we find a testament to the enduring interplay of human agency and the greater cosmic currents that shape the course of events.

Aeroplanes

Isaiah 31:1-6 reads, "As birds flying, so will the Lord of hosts defend Jerusalem; defending also he will deliver it; and passing over he will preserve it. Turn ye unto him from whom the children of Israel have deeply revolted."

In the pages of Isaiah 31:1-6, a vivid tableau unfolds, resplendent with the imagery of birds taking to the skies as harbingers of divine protection and guidance. This scripture not only captures a poignant message of reassurance but also encapsulates the profound historical journey of Israel, a narrative that unfolds with echoes of divine intervention and human agency.

Verse 5, akin to the graceful flight of birds soaring across the heavens, paints a vivid picture of the Lord of hosts as the vigilant guardian of Jerusalem. Just as these winged creatures navigate the skies with precision, so shall the Almighty safeguard the city, ensuring its defense, deliverance, and preservation. This imagery carries with it a palpable sense of divine watchfulness, evoking a profound sense of protection that stretches beyond the tangible realm.

Amid the backdrop of this celestial protection, verse 6 invites us to reflect on the intricate relationship between divine call and human response. A call to "Turn ye unto him" resonates, beckoning the children of Israel to realign their path, casting aside the shackles of deep-seated rebellion. This spiritual turning, an embrace of divine ways, emerges as a transformative act—one that embodies the essence of repentance and reconnection.

Amid these verses lies the historical tapestry of Israel—a journey marked by trials, triumphs, and a covenant woven with promises. The ebb and flow of Israel's history, punctuated by moments of divine guidance and human choices, find resonance within the verses. The land of Israel, granted by God, witnessed the unfolding of a complex narrative—an intricate dance between divine providence and human response.

The scriptural narrative echoes the resonance of Israel's history, where rebellion led to exile—a painful rupture from the land bestowed to them. Idolatry, a betrayal of the sacred covenant, resulted in the unravelling of their connection to the very land that was meant to be their sanctuary. Yet, within this ebb, the promise of return stood unshaken—a testament to God's unwavering faithfulness and the immutable nature of His covenant.

The return of Israel, akin to emerging from the depths of Egypt, symbolizes a new chapter—a reclamation of their rightful heritage. Just as the Israelites journeyed from Egypt to claim the land promised to them, the historical landscape took on new contours with the advent of General Allenby. His symbolic journey echoed this profound narrative—a liberation that transcended the physical and embraced the spiritual.

In the annals of history, General Allenby's journey mirrored a larger narrative—a resonating call of destiny, redemption, and the fulfillment of divine promise. The echoes of Israel's journey, spanning the pages of scripture and history, resonated with a shared trajectory of liberation, restoration, and divine watchfulness. Within the tapestry of Isaiah 31:1-6, we find an intricate mosaic—a fusion of scripture and history—inviting us to reflect on the intricate interplay of divine orchestration and human response, as well as the eternal promise that unfurls across time and space.

Israel was kicked out of the land of Israel because they revolted against God who gave them the land because of Idolatry of the people of the land. Now because of their idolatry Israel was kicked out themselves but God promised them to return. Obviously, God cannot lie and His promises cannot fail! Israel comes out of Egypt to conquer the land! Allenby comes out of Egypt!

Edmund Allenby,
1st Viscount Allenby

Field Marshal Edmund Henry Hynman Allenby, 1st Viscount Allenby, GCB, GCMG, GCVO, was a prominent English soldier known for his roles in the Second Boer War and the First World War. Born on April 23, 1861, Allenby's influence spans pivotal conflicts in history.

In the First World War, he led the British Empire's Egyptian Expeditionary Force (EEF) during the Sinai and Palestine Campaign against the Ottoman Empire, leaving an indelible mark on the course of history.

General Allenby's significance extends to the symbolism of Great Britain and Israel, embodying their valor and aspirations. As the lion and its young symbolize these nations, Allenby's leadership mirrors their courage and dedication.

His legacy remains a beacon of courage and leadership, inspiring generations and underscoring the power of individuals to shape history.

Royal Coat of Arms of the United Kingdom

I've previously delved into the distinct tribes of Israel in more comprehensive discussions. To put it succinctly, the lion, the Unicorn, and the Harp symbolize Israel and Juda, as evident in Numbers 24:8, Deuteronomy 33:17, 20, 22, 29, Psalm 22:21, and Psalm 92:10.

This symbolism becomes more apparent when observing the Royal Coat of Arms of the UK, where the representations of Ephraim, Manasseh, King David's harp, and the Unicorn's horns converge. The alignment of these elements isn't a mere coincidence; rather, it holds deeper significance.

Interestingly, the UK also harbors influences from the tribe of Dan, and traces of Gad are evident through historical associations. This is reflected in how the title of "Gotha" was once borne by the King of England.

By recognizing these connections, we gain insight into why I assert that the UK stands as a representative of the tribes of Israel. The same principle applies to the USA, as well as the original tribes of South Africa (European descendants) and Australia / New Zealand.

To come back to aeroplanes let us see what Isaiah 31:5 means; "As birds flying, so will the Lord of hosts defend Jerusalem; defending also he will deliver it; and passing over he will preserve it."

As we have seen general Allenby walked into Jerusalem but some other very interesting things happened there.

Allenby and "Allah Beh"

In 1917, under the command of British General Edmund Allenby, troops converged to encircle the city of Jerusalem. It is recounted that on the eve of his impending invasion, Allenby fervently prayed for a victory that wouldn't harm the sacred sites of the city. Seeking guidance, he reached out to London for counsel and received a response that was both simple and profound—a scripture verse. Isaiah 31:5 declared, "As birds flying, so will the LORD of hosts defend Jerusalem; defending also he will deliver it; and passing over he will preserve it."

Filled with the promising prospects of this revelation, Allenby orchestrated the reading of the verse before his assembled forces stationed in the foothills of Jerusalem. What followed was a remarkable spectacle—an aerial display that resonated with divine symbolism. Allenby mobilized every available aircraft for a sweeping fly-over. As the sun dawned on December 10, a multitude of planes gracefully skimmed the skies, their wings stretching in a formation that seemed endless. Over the "Hill of Evil Council," situated south of the Temple site, the aircraft descended with grace. The atmosphere buzzed with the hum of engines as British biplanes, alongside captured German aircraft and various flying machines, united in a breathtaking display that filled the sky from wingtip to wingtip, from nose to tail.

This spectacular tribute to the heavens became a testament to Allenby's deep faith and his conviction to approach the sacred task at hand with reverence. The verse that guided his intentions now adorned the sky with wings of hope and protection, a celestial embrace of the city that had witnessed millennia of history and significance.

Submarines

During the tumultuous era of the First World War, a significant transformation in naval warfare was spearheaded by the strategic deployment of submarines. These underwater vessels, harnessed by the German government, proved to be instrumental in reshaping the dynamics of the conflict. Originally designed to target warships, submarines found their true potency in targeting merchant shipping as the war's trajectory evolved. However, this shift in strategy was not without diplomatic consequences, triggering diplomatic crises with neutral nations and, ultimately, leading to the involvement of the United States.

Throughout the war, German submarines exerted a profound influence on maritime engagements. Their impact was palpable, as these vessels managed to sink an impressive total of 6,394 ships, collectively displacing a staggering 11,948,702 tons. This audacious campaign came at a cost, with Germany losing 229 submarines in the process. The average tonnage sunk per submarine, nearly 52,000 tons, attests to their potency as a disruptive force in naval warfare.

Nonetheless, the culmination of the submarine campaign did not solely determine the war's outcome. While they left an indelible mark on naval operations, their role was more transformative than decisive. Their actions precipitated a pivotal turning point—the entry of the United States into the conflict, altering the course of the war's geopolitical dynamics.

The convergence of submarine warfare and the broader context of the First World War resonates as a potent example of technological advancement intersecting with strategic choices. These underwater vessels, navigating beneath the surface, serve as a metaphor for the hidden currents of warfare and the unforeseen consequences of strategic decisions.

As we reflect on the historical significance of submarines, a parallel emerges with prophetic references found within biblical scriptures. Their emergence as a formidable and far-reaching force parallels the symbolic imagery found in these texts. The interplay between historical events and scriptural narratives underscores the intricate tapestry of human history intertwined with divine intent. The profound implications of submarines align with the enigmatic themes found within the pages of Revelation.

In summation, our exploration underscores the multifaceted connections between the First World War and the prophecies of Revelation. While this analysis offers a focused perspective, it highlights factors linking WW1 to the symbolic first trumpet. The thunderous echoes of artillery and the strategic shifts of global power find resonance in the scriptural imagery of Revelation 8:7.

SECTION 2

THE SECOND ANGEL SOUNDED:- WW2

Revelation 8:8-9 reads, "And the second angel sounded, and as it were a great mountain burning with fire was cast into the sea: and the third part of the sea became blood; And the third part of the creatures which were in the sea, and had life, died; and the third part of the ships were destroyed."

Most of the Bible translations talks about fishes but that is a wrong interpretation! You cannot count the fishes in the sea but you can count the submarines. The ships were man-made objects and countable and so for the submarines!

Let us not try to read things into the bible that are not there, nor try to take things out of the Word that is there. It is one very dangerous habit of changing The Word of God to suit you! See Revelation 22:18.

Revelation 22:18 reads, "For I testify unto every man that heareth the words of the prophecy of this book, If any man shall add unto these things, God shall add unto him the plagues that are written in this book."

Strong's Concordance: 2938. Ktisma = a created thing, a creature.

Thayer's Greek Lexicon: STRONGS NT 2938: κτίσμα - thing founded; created thing.

A ship and a submarine are created things and they were destroyed or perished away, a third of each. Both in verse 9 of Revelation 8.

Now the main part of the second world war was about the fight to control of the Atlantic Ocean and the seas surrounding The British Isles and Germany. The reason for this is plain to see; Neither Germany or Britain was able to support themselves apart from imports like food and industrial supplies for their war efforts. Therefore, both tried to cut off the other's supply of ships with food and war machines and anything else needed for the war effort and survival. Britain declared war on Germany before they were ready for war. Hitler planned for Germany to be rearmed by around 1945. They were not fully rearmed after the Treaty of Versailles after WW1.

The Treaty of Versailles

The Treaty of Versailles, known as "Traité de Versailles" in French and "Versailler Vertrag" in German, marked a pivotal juncture in history as the paramount peace treaty that effectively concluded the tumultuous era of World War I.

As can be seen above Germany was forced to accept total responsibility for WW1 and heavily penalised for that. Anybody knows it takes two to tango. That gave rise to the Nazi Party's success in the 1930's. And the International Bankers had a field day. They had branches of their banks n Britain and Germany and the USA and everywhere else. The warring nations spent money like water during the wars but the national debts remained. And obviously the taxes were increased to cover the debts and immediately plans were made for the next war to make more money for the industrialists and bankers. In this way small businesses were kept off their feet and not able to accumulate capital. The whole idea is to make sure that the power stays in the hands of big business and the International Bankers and Big Industry. The small man must never get a big slice of the cake. He has to be kept off his feet unable to accumulate capital. More power to the main players. The New World Order.

We have some background now of the WW2. The mountain of fire cast into the sea is the same fire as in WW1 under the previous chapter. Fire and brimstone out of the cannons or guns at sea. And the mountain of angelic forces. Blood in the sea is human blood that came from the war at sea; ships and submarines and aeroplanes. All the weapons drew blood. A third part means the area of the war zone, not the whole world or all the seas.

A Third Part of the Ships and Submarines were Destroyed

My belief is that a significant fraction, approximately one-third, of the ships actively engaged in naval operations during World War II suffered destruction. However, this impact was not limited to surface vessels alone; submarines, which played a pivotal role in naval warfare, also experienced a similar fate during the chaotic battles at sea. Both ships and submarines, despite being human-made creations, held immense strategic importance, as they were essential for transporting vital supplies and military strength across the vast expanse of the ocean.

Submarines underwent a remarkable transformation in World War II compared to their predecessors in World War I. They gained higher speeds, more powerful weapons, advanced detection technology, and newfound flexibility. Instead of merely waiting for opportunities, these submarines became proactive in engaging their targets, reshaping their role from passive ambush to active participation in combat. Historian Gary E. Weir pointed out that submarines had evolved into a crucial force that significantly impacted the war's course.

A prime example of submarine effectiveness was the German submarine U-48, a Type VIIB U-boat commissioned by Nazi Germany's Kriegsmarine. U-48's remarkable accomplishments during its two-year active service stand as a testament to the potency of these underwater vessels. Over twelve war patrols, U-48 sunk an impressive 51 ships, amounting to 299,477 GRT (gross register tonnage), and damaged an additional four ships, accounting for 27,877 GRT.

A Great Mountain Burning with Fire was Cast into the Sea

In the pages of history, an awe-inspiring spectacle unfolds—a vivid portrayal of a great mountain ablaze with fire, dramatically cast into the vast expanse of the sea. The nuances of this event carry layers of significance, both in their literal interpretation and their symbolic resonance.

Delving into the linguistic essence, we uncover the term "oros" (ὄρος), which encapsulates the image of a mountain, a soaring hill that reaches toward the heavens. This visual is imbued with power and grandeur, evoking a sense of awe that has echoed through the ages.

Interwoven with "hós" (ὡς), which translates to "as" or "like as," the narrative takes on a dynamic quality. The fusion of these words paints a vivid picture of the mountain, not merely as a static entity, but as a dynamic force embodying fire and energy, descending upon the sea with profound impact.

Intriguingly, high explosives emerge as a central player in this maritime saga, akin to a symphony of destruction and chaos. The explosive might of these devices becomes a defining element, orchestrating a cataclysmic dance between fire and water. With precision, the bombs strike their intended targets, triggering a remarkable phenomenon—an eruption of fire, akin to a majestic mountain enveloped in flames.

The interlinear Bible, a gateway to deeper comprehension, unfolds a striking revelation. It speaks of a "great mountain with fire burning" being cast into the sea—a moment of intensity and transformation. The symbolism here transcends the literal, reflecting a pivotal event in the tides of history, where fire meets water in a dramatic clash.

The resonance extends beyond the surface, echoing the tumultuous battles that characterized naval warfare. Just as fire engulfs the mountain, so too did the flames of war envelop the seas. The imagery encapsulates the explosive nature of conflict, where the clash of opposing forces mirrors the collision of fire and water.

See scenes from Pearl Harbor:
https://edition.cnn.com/2022/12/07/us/gallery/pearl-harbor-attack/index.html

Battle of the Atlantic

the Battle of the Atlantic took center stage from 1939 to 1945—a sustained military campaign during World War II that spanned a significant portion of naval history within this period. This engagement primarily revolved around the Allied naval blockade of Germany, established immediately after the war declaration, and Germany's subsequent counter-blockade in response. The pinnacle of this campaign occurred between 1940 and 1943.

Additionally, the conclusion of the war brought forth pivotal moments in the form of the Hiroshima and Nagasaki bombings. The reference to a "great mountain burning with fire cast into the sea" could be seen as a symbolic description of these events, representing the cataclysmic impact of nuclear weaponry.

The sea war was the most significant element of WW2 and that is why the bible calls attention to it in the Second Trumpet!

SECTION 3

THE THIRD ANGEL SOUNDED: THE WORMWOOD PROPHESY

Revelation 8:10-11 reads, "And the third angel sounded, and there fell a great star from heaven, burning as it were a lamp, and it fell upon the third part of the rivers, and upon the fountains of waters; And the name of the star is called Wormwood: and the third part of the waters became wormwood; and many men died of the waters, because they were made bitter."

The Wormwood Prophecy

The Wormwood prophecy is a focal point that we'll explore within the broader context of historical events. Our journey spans from World War I to World War II and extends into the Cold War, an extension of the second global conflict. Despite their collaboration during WWII, the United States and the USSR found themselves embroiled in a power struggle fueled by the arms race and ideological differences during the Cold War era. The backdrop of these events sets the stage for understanding the significance of the Wormwood prophecy in Revelation.

The Cold War Era

The Cold War emerged as a continuation of the global power dynamics established in the aftermath of World War II. The USA, now a formidable world power, engaged in a complex relationship with the USSR. Despite their wartime alliance, the post-war landscape saw the USA supporting the USSR with war supplies. This inadvertently fostered an arms race as the USA's technological advancements were funneled to the USSR, pushing them to compete. However, the foundation of communism and socialism became apparent – they relied on external support, much like a red horse that needs sustenance.

Tensions escalated as communist espionage infiltrated various spheres, exemplified by figures like Alger Hiss. This period marked a transition from direct military confrontations to ideological battles, laying the groundwork for the eventual fall of the Berlin Wall.

The Berlin Wall and the Shofar President Ronald Reagan's iconic speech on June 12, 1987, encapsulated the culmination of the Cold War. He challenged Soviet Leader Mikhail Gorbachev to "tear down" the Berlin Wall, a potent symbol of division in Germany's Communist era. This marked a pivotal moment that preceded another significant event associated with the Wormwood prophecy.

Chernobyl: The Wormwood Event

The Third Trumpet of Revelation introduces the concept of Wormwood, a term that takes on profound meaning in the context of the Chernobyl disaster. The Power Station of Chernobyl derives its name from the Ukrainian word for Artemisia vulgaris, commonly known as mugwort or wormwood. The Power station's name signifies the darker variety of this plant, as opposed to the lighter-stemmed A. absinthium.

The Chernobyl disaster unfolded as a catastrophic nuclear accident in 1986, releasing unprecedented levels of radiation. This incident took on the significance of Wormwood, a harbinger of disaster, aligning with the Third Trumpet in Revelation. The term "Chernobyl" itself embodies the concept of Wormwood in Russian, underscoring the prophetic nature of this event.

The Wormwood prophecy encapsulates a chain of events that traverse historical periods, revealing a tapestry of interconnectedness between global conflicts and spiritual symbolism. As we explore the interplay between world affairs and prophetic revelation, we find compelling correlations that underscore the timeless relevance of scripture in understanding our complex world.

So now we have identified Wormwood as Chernobyl let us look at what happened there.

Chernobyl Nuclear Reactor Disaster

On April 26, 1986, an unprecedented catastrophe unfolded as one of the reactors at the Chernobyl Nuclear Power Plant experienced a catastrophic explosion. The event was triggered by unauthorized experiments conducted by plant operators, resulting in a catastrophic loss of control. This disaster was underpinned by significant design flaws inherent in the RBMK reactor, which rendered it unstable when operated at low power. This instability paved the way for a perilous phenomenon known as thermal runaway, where rising temperatures amplified reactor power output to dangerous levels.

In the aftermath of the explosion, Chernobyl Power Plant found itself at the epicenter of a dire situation. As a result of the disaster's severity, Pripyat city was evacuated just nine days later. The evacuation served as a response to the unprecedented levels of contamination, particularly from caesium-137. This radioactive isotope posed severe health risks, prompting the need for immediate and decisive action.

The extent of contamination was quantified through the presence of caesium-137, with a surface ground deposition in 1986 measuring around 555 kilobecquerels per square meter (kBq/m2). This measurement serves as a grim reminder of the far-reaching impact of the disaster on the environment and the potential hazards it posed to human health.

'Monument of the Third Angel'

The biblical sculpture at Chernobyl's 'Wormwood Star Memorial Complex' stands as a tribute to the lives, homes, and communities lost to the disaster. Created by Ukrainian artist Anatoly Haidamaka, the sculpture features a lone angel with a trumpet, representing the victims of one of the world's worst nuclear catastrophes. Positioned at the entrance, this artwork symbolizes both mourning and hope, embodying the resilience and unity of humanity in the face of adversity.

The angel backdropped by a sea of stars. DARMON RICHTER/USED WITH PERMISSION

Wormwood

Hebrew "la'anah" refers to Artemisia absinthium in botanical terms. This plant is renowned for its remarkably strong bitterness, as mentioned in Deuteronomy 29:18, Proverbs 5:4, Jeremiah 9:15, and Amos 5:7. It symbolizes bitterness, affliction, remorse, and punitive suffering. In Amos 6:12, this Hebrew term is translated as "hemlock" in the Revised Version (RV), though it's commonly rendered as "wormwood."

In the symbolic language of the Book of Revelation (Revelation 8:10, 11), a falling star poisons the earth's waters, causing a third of the water to become as bitter as wormwood.

The Greek term for this plant, "absinthion," literally means "undrinkable." The absinthe in France is distilled from a specific species of this plant. Additionally, another species of it known as "southernwood" or "old man" is grown in cottage gardens due to its pleasant aroma.

There it is: plain as day! Absinthion means undrinkable! Let us now consider the effects of Chernobyl had on the waters of Europe!

Effects of the Chernobyl disaster

The catastrophic Chernobyl disaster, which occurred in 1986, had devastating consequences, leading to the release of significant quantities of radioactive contamination into the atmosphere in the form of both particulate matter and gaseous radioisotopes. This event stands as the most substantial unintentional emission of radioactivity into the environment to date, a distinction it continues to hold as of 2021.

The work conducted by the Scientific Committee on Problems of the Environment (SCOPE) has emphasized the complexity of comparing the Chernobyl incident with atmospheric nuclear weapon tests through a simple assessment of being better or worse. This intricate comparison is due in part to the nature of the isotopes released during the Chernobyl disaster, which were characterized by longer half-lives compared to those liberated by atomic bomb detonations.

The economic repercussions stemming from this disaster are staggering, estimated at a monumental $235 billion in damages. This figure highlights the extensive impact not only on human lives but also on infrastructural and environmental well-being.

During the aftermath of the explosion, those who became known as the "liquidators" and firefighters displayed immense bravery, stepping into the unknown radiation hazards to control the fire. Tragically, many of them succumbed to radiation-related health issues, falling victim while heroically battling the inferno. It is a poignant reminder of the profound risks faced by those on the front lines of such catastrophes.

Regrettably, the long-term effects of the Chernobyl disaster were downplayed by Russia and much of the media, leaving a cloud of misinformation and underestimation hovering over the true extent of the aftermath. This underreporting has, in some ways, hindered a comprehensive understanding of the disaster's full impact.

Interestingly, the Bible contains a metaphor that resonates with the scale of contamination witnessed in Chernobyl. In its language, it speaks of a third of the water being tainted, an eerily resonant description of the ecological upheaval and contamination caused by such a monumental event.

To fully comprehend the lasting implications of the Chernobyl disaster, it's crucial to seek out substantiated evidence that sheds light on its long-term effects on both the environment and human health.

Radiation Doses in Europe After the Chernobyl Accident

Following the catastrophic Chernobyl accident in 1986, Europe bore the brunt of the aftermath's radiation doses. The reactor malfunction resulted in the release of substantial quantities of radioactive materials, which spread across Europe and even reached other parts of the world.

The event itself took place on April 26, 1986, at the No. 4 reactor within the Chernobyl Nuclear Power Plant, situated near the city of Pripyat in the northern region of the Ukrainian SSR in the Soviet Union. This disaster has earned the grim distinction of being the most severe nuclear accident in history, both in terms of its economic toll and the human casualties it inflicted. Its severity ranks at the highest level of seven on the International Nuclear Event Scale, the same ranking shared by only one other incident: the 2011 Fukushima Daiichi nuclear disaster in Japan.

In response to the immediate emergency and the subsequent need for environmental decontamination, an impressive workforce of over 500,000 personnel was involved. This monumental effort, along with the decontamination process, incurred an estimated cost of around 18 billion Soviet rubles—equivalent to approximately $68 billion in 2019 when adjusted for inflation. This colossal financial expenditure underscores the immense scale of the disaster's impact.

It's no exaggeration to state that this disaster stands as the most catastrophic nuclear event in history. The magnitude of its consequences is so profound that it's no surprise that even the Bible references it, highlighting the gravity and enduring significance of the Chernobyl disaster.

So where was the witness in heaven, Halley's Comet, at that moment in time? It should have been around a while as a sign!

So, where exactly was the celestial witness, Halley's Comet, positioned in the heavens at that crucial moment in time? One might expect this comet, with its historical significance as a herald, to have been present for a while as an unmistakable sign.

Halley's Comet, scientifically designated as 1P/Halley, is a short-period comet that graces Earth's vicinity approximately every 75 to 76 years. This celestial phenomenon possesses a unique distinction: it's one of the few short-period comets visible to the unaided eye from our planet, and hence, the only one that can make two appearances within a single human lifespan. The comet last made its inner Solar System appearance in 1986 and is projected to reappear around mid-2061.

Remarkably, during its 1986 manifestation, Halley's Comet earned the distinction of being the first comet subjected to close scrutiny by spacecraft, yielding unprecedented insights into the structure of a comet nucleus and the processes underlying the formation of its coma and tail. This momentous occasion marked a turning point in our understanding of cometary construction, substantiating theories such as Fred Whipple's "dirty snowball" model. This model accurately predicted Halley's composition, a mix of volatile ices—like water, carbon dioxide, ammonia—and dust. However, these missions also caused significant revision of these concepts, revealing that the comet's surface is predominantly comprised of non-volatile, dusty materials, with only a fraction being icy.

Evident from the records, Comet 1P/Halley was not only visibly discernible to the unaided eye, but it also garnered the attention of Russian satellites. As captured in the image taken on March 8, 1986, by W. Liller from Easter Island—part of the International Halley Watch (IHW) Large Scale Phenomena Network—the comet's appearance was an awe-inspiring spectacle.

Interestingly, Halley's Comet's visibility to the naked eye was complemented by the in-depth observations carried out by Russian spacecraft. It's worth noting that this celestial entity, with its brilliance akin to a burning star, has been linked to Revelation 10:8, symbolizing a radiant lamp.

Halley's Comet as photographed May 8, 1910

This photo is in the public Domain. Everything before 1926 is not subject to copyright. However, the picture tells it's own story. It still looks like a burning lamp and it was visible with the naked eye during the Chernobyl disaster.

Halley's Comet as photographed May 8, 1910 by NASA

File: Halley's Comet - May 29 1910.jpg - Wikimedia Commons

The comet was not only a subject of observation from Earth but also from the vantage point of Russian spacecraft nearby.

Something very interesting has happened just recently:

Russo-Ukrainian War

Ukraine is a democracy and Russia is not. Putin has been in power now for 22 years and he wants the old USSR back! That's not democracy. But what happened to Chernobyl?

The Russo-Ukrainian War has unveiled the stark contrast between Ukraine's democratic framework and Russia's autocratic regime, led by Putin for over two decades. Amid this geopolitical turmoil, a shadow looms from the past: the Chernobyl disaster.

A curious twist unfolds as we delve into the annals of the Russian invasion of Ukraine. Astonishingly, on the very first day of this invasion, Russian forces set their sights on the exclusion zone encompassing the eerie remnants of Pripyat and Chernobyl. The question beckons: what motivates this audacious move? Despite the evident peril buried beneath the old reactor's protective dome—an accumulation of nuclear fuel—Russian forces seem undeterred. This stockpile of nuclear energy lies dormant yet potent, a potential threat for generations to come.

The dome erected to enclose Chernobyl's radiation remains a testament to human effort, yet its age hints at vulnerability. Nuclear reactions within its confines persist, the radioactive materials lingering and potentially retaining their power for centuries—or in the worst-case scenario, mere days. This precarious situation fuels unease, spelling impending trouble on the horizon.

The paradox deepens as we consider Ukraine's moniker as the "bread basket of Europe." Fertile lands surround Chernobyl, but their bounty is tainted by radioactive contamination, rendering the produce unsafe for consumption. Beneath the soil, the legacy of 1986 seeps into European waters, an ongoing reminder of a disaster that continues to reverberate.

The far-reaching implications become evident even in faraway lands like South Africa, where corn tainted with elevated radiation levels from Ukraine's contaminated soils makes its way onto the dinner plates. The impact is visceral—produce meant for sustenance now carries the burdensome legacy of nuclear catastrophe.

The enigma surrounding Chernobyl deepens when we trace its origins. It wasn't just a power plant; it held a strategic purpose—feeding electricity to the Russian spy radar of the era, known as the Duga radar. This colossal Soviet installation, nestled in the forests of northern Ukraine, was constructed during the height of the Cold War. The Duga radar remains shrouded in mystery, a stark reminder of the ideological struggles that once gripped the world.

The symbiotic relationship between Duga and Chernobyl becomes evident. When Chernobyl's reactor catastrophically failed, the repercussions rippled far beyond the immediate disaster. The explosion of Chernobyl's nuclear power plant metaphorically mirrored the implosion of the USSR itself, a defining moment in the Cold War's narrative.

Chernobyl: How Gorbachev Claimed Disaster was REAL Reason Behind Soviet Union's Collapse

Mikhail Gorbachev, the final leader of the Soviet Union, positioned himself as a reformer, aiming to modernize and revitalize the crumbling Soviet system. His introduction of Glasnost, a policy fostering greater openness to Western influences, and Perestroika, a bold endeavor to restructure the stagnant Soviet economy, were emblematic of his aspirations for change.

However, the Chernobyl catastrophe marked a turning point that laid bare the hollowness of these reforms. The harrowing event, compounded by a futile attempt to conceal the magnitude of the disaster, punctured the facade of Glasnost's promises. The ruling party's reluctance to embrace true transparency became glaringly evident, shattering the credibility of their professed intentions.

The devastating aftermath of Chernobyl, a nuclear calamity that sent shockwaves across the globe, served as a stark revelation. In a revealing 2006 interview, Gorbachev himself acknowledged the profound impact of the disaster, stating: "The nuclear meltdown at Chernobyl 20 years ago this month, even more than my launch of Perestroika, was perhaps the real cause of the collapse of the Soviet Union five years later."

This statement encapsulated the seismic role Chernobyl played in the annihilation of the Soviet Union. Beyond the physical destruction and radiological fallout, the disaster's ripple effects illuminated the deep-seated issues plaguing the Soviet leadership. The collision between Gorbachev's aspirations for renewal and the grim reality of systemic flaws became undeniable, ultimately eroding the regime's legitimacy and precipitating its downfall.

The Chernobyl catastrophe was not merely a nuclear incident; it was a metaphorical meltdown of the Soviet Union's already fragile foundations. Gorbachev's earnest intentions, exemplified by his reformist policies, were overshadowed by the undeniable consequences of the disaster. The disparity between his vision and the regime's actions, starkly exposed by Chernobyl's aftermath, cast an indelible shadow over the Soviet Union's trajectory.

So where is Putin on this topic?

Putin Warns of Tough Russian Action if West Crosses 'red line'

Russian President Vladimir Putin's recent warning about the consequences of the West crossing a metaphorical "red line" has stirred intrigue and speculation. Employing words like "asymmetrical, rapid, and harsh" to describe the potential response raises questions about the motivations behind such rhetoric and the historical context in which it is framed.

Delving into the layers of Putin's message, one cannot help but ponder whether this is a strategic maneuver to harken back to the ideological foundations that sustained the former USSR. The resonance of Marxist values and a desire to reclaim the expansive reach the USSR once held might be driving Putin's intentions. Yet, this intricate tapestry of geopolitical motives remains a subject best left to the meticulous hands of historians.

However, the alignment of these events with scriptural narratives is intriguing. Reflecting upon the Third trumpet of the Chernobyl disaster and its enduring aftermath, one also witnesses the subsequent fall of the USSR—a precursor to the current dynamics. Putin's recalibration, observed through the lens of prophetic speculation, could be indicative of a regrouping for the upcoming and climactic 7th trumpet. This scenario gives rise to speculation about Ukraine, possibly serving as one of the symbolic "ribs" in the grasp of the Russian Bear—a foreboding image from scripture.

If Russia's reach extends to claim two more such metaphorical "ribs," it could mark a definitive step towards fulfilling prophecy. A pivotal notion is the potential aspiration for Russia to integrate into the NATO alliance—a precursor to its anticipated role in the emerging Holy Roman Empire. A union that will inevitably span all of Europe, encompassing even Russia itself. The prospect of seizing Ukraine aligns with Putin's aspirations to hold a prominent seat in the European theater.

A historical backdrop underscores the relentless pursuit of power by communist regimes, epitomized by the staggering human toll taken to establish their supremacy. This legacy might be driving Russia's resolve to undermine democracies, emphasizing the perceived failings of democratic systems and championing communism as the ultimate path to global dominance—the New World Order. The fulfillment of such ambitions, however, might only come to fruition after the cataclysmic 7th trumpet and the impending Armageddon.

Amid this intricate dance between ideologies, the convergence of democracies and various forms of communism—echoing Daniel's prophecies—becomes increasingly pronounced. Swiftly, the pieces fall into place, offering a glimpse into a future that seems to be hurdling toward realization. Russia's symbolic double-headed eagle, reminiscent of the Holy Roman Empire, aligns with its emblematic bear, suggesting an intricate dance between history and prophecy.

Cancer incidence and mortality patterns in Europe: Estimates for 40 countries and 25 major cancers in 2018

A puzzling and concerning phenomenon emerges from the realm of cancer statistics: Europe, while housing a mere 9% of the global population, shoulders an astounding 25% share of the worldwide cancer burden. This staggering disparity calls for a profound examination, as it has far-reaching implications for healthcare planning and resource allocation. These cancer statistics, serving as a bellwether of societal health, underscore the urgency of informed strategies to combat this rising challenge.

The importance of up-to-date cancer data cannot be overstated. These statistics form the bedrock upon which cancer planning strategies are meticulously crafted. They serve as the guiding light for healthcare professionals, policymakers, and researchers, illuminating the path toward effective prevention, diagnosis, and treatment of this formidable adversary.

Comprehensive cancer data, spanning 25 major types of cancers, have been meticulously gathered for 40 countries across the four delineated regions of Europe as defined by the United Nations. The comprehensive scope of these efforts, encapsulating the entirety of

Europe and the European Union (EU-28) for the year 2018, provides a panoramic view of the cancer landscape. These statistics are indispensable tools, empowering stakeholders with the knowledge needed to navigate the intricate challenges posed by this complex ailment.

Could these statistics simply be figures on a page, devoid of meaning? The answer, in all likelihood, is a resounding no. This assertion gains gravitas when we consider the profound impact of groundwater radiation. The nexus between environmental factors, such as radiation exposure, and cancer incidence cannot be ignored. Could groundwater radiation, influenced by multiple variables including historical events like Chernobyl, be a silent contributor to the disparities observed in cancer burdens across Europe?

Remarkably, ancient wisdom surfaces in this context. The biblical perspective sheds light on the interconnectedness of health and environment. Groundwater, known as a life-sustaining source, might also bear the weight of unseen influences, possibly reflected in these statistics. These interwoven layers of insight inspire deeper contemplation, bridging scientific investigation with historical context.

The convergence of scientific inquiry and ancient wisdom offers a nuanced perspective. As we strive to decipher the intricate web of cancer's origins and implications, the biblical references serve as a reminder that health, environment, and societal well-being are deeply intertwined. This amalgamation of modern research and age-old wisdom serves as a testament to the multifaceted nature of human health—a mosaic in which statistics are but fragments of a grander narrative.

Conclusion Wormwood

Within the realm of perception lies a conviction that the true extent of damage inflicted by the Chernobyl disaster has already been etched into history. Framing this assertion is the evocative biblical imagery of "a third of the water became bitter, like wormwood," reminiscent of Chernobyl or Chornobyl—a name that resonates with haunting echoes. This reference, often overlooked, encapsulates a sobering truth: the scope of the tragedy's ramifications encompasses not just a localized disaster, but an extensive geographic expanse. This imagery reveals that approximately a third of Europe, which bore the brunt of radioactive fallout, became entwined in the crisis.

The unfolding of the disaster unfolded like a dark symphony—radioactive particles descending from the skies, intermingling with rainstorms, and casting their ominous shadow over vast stretches of land. The rainstorms, acting as unwitting conduits, ushered the radioactivity downward, seeping it into the very essence of the earth: the underground water. This hidden aquifer, cloaked beneath the surface, became an unwitting bearer of the unseen, channeling its influence into the plants, grass, wheat, and even the radiant sunflowers that painted the landscape.

The intricate cycle continued as the affected flora took their place in the delicate dance of life. Cows and sheep grazed upon this altered vegetation, their very existence entwined with the tainted sustenance.

The repercussions extended beyond the surface—wool, milk, and other byproducts bore the indelible mark of the catastrophe. Even the reaches of the United Kingdom felt the ripples of Chernobyl's impact, a testament to the far-reaching nature of this silent crisis.

The Ukrainian connection, however, remains particularly poignant. Its products, though separated by geography, remain bound by the tragic tendrils of radioactivity. Evident even today, packaging proclaims a radiation level surpassing the norm—a silent testament to the resilience of history's scars.

Yet, the response to this subtle menace is peculiarly human— enveloped in hushed conversations, concealed truths, and an unspoken wish that avoidance equates to resolution. The belief that the act of evading discussion could render a problem null is reminiscent of the sentiment that if the name of God is left unspoken, His presence will fade into obscurity. But just as the divine presence defies invisibility, so too does the enduring legacy of Chernobyl. It is etched in history, in the testimony of the land, and in the hushed whispers of those who remember.

In this interplay of terrestrial and ethereal, the biblical references resonate with poignant clarity. The message is clear: a silent crisis cannot be undone by averting the gaze. And just as the testament of Christ's presence endures through centuries, so does the memory of Chernobyl—the unseen threads woven into the tapestry of human existence.

Aftermath

The specter of Chernobyl Reactor No. 4 looms ominously, shrouded in the disconcerting shadows of uncertainty. Its very core, a cauldron of nuclear fuel, stands as an enigmatic enigma that resists the probing gaze of human intervention. It's a conundrum, poised within the reactor's confines, that not even the boldest among us can fathom to approach. The potential implications of this unapproachability beckon contemplation—could the lurking truths behind this veil of opacity remain forever out of reach?

Amidst this veil of ambiguity, a question emerges—a question that resonates not just within the confines of one individual's mind, but across the collective consciousness of those who grapple with the legacy of Chernobyl. Could the notion of placing measuring instruments within the core's depths be relegated to mere fantasy? The opacity surrounding this proposition raises more queries than it resolves, serving as a testament to the complexity of nuclear mysteries.

Turning our gaze to the protective dome enveloping the sarcophagus, hope emerges as a fragile beacon. This colossal structure, akin to a sentinel guarding against catastrophic release, holds the potential to thwart another perilous explosion. With bated breath, we yearn for its resilience to endure, echoing in the chambers of our prayers that it remains impervious to the forces that once ravaged its predecessor.

The aftermath of Chernobyl's No. 4 reactor explosion delivered an unsettling legacy, fraught with unanticipated consequences. The tempestuous storms that ensued following the catastrophe played an unforeseen role—transforming rain into a vector of contamination. The cascading raindrops, unwitting couriers of radioactive particles, orchestrated the dissemination of contamination deep into the earth, infiltrating the groundwater that courses beneath the lands.

The repercussions of this subterranean contamination stretch into the horizon, spanning not just years, but centuries—a tapestry woven with the intricacies of radioactive influence. The stark reality is that even today, products emanating from Russia and its satellites bear the silent signature of elevated radiation levels. A grim economic underbelly exists, one where clandestine dealings wield Rubles beneath the table, bending norms to greed's will. But let us not forget that even the most impenetrable fortresses can be eroded when ambition and desperation align.

In the realm of geopolitical power plays, even the megalithic city of Moscow bows to the decree—contaminated corn, rendered toxic by history's tragedies, meets stern orders against its sale within its hallowed precincts.

As we traverse the corridors of human history, we encounter conundrums that transcend boundaries and epochs. The tale of Chernobyl, a parable of uncharted territories, teaches us that some enigmas might remain veiled, even as they shape the course of our shared destiny.

Forsmark: how Sweden alerted the world about the danger of the Chernobyl disaster

Nestled within the pages of history lies the chronicle of Forsmark—a pivotal chapter that unravels the tale of how Sweden's vigilant watchfulness served as a beacon of warning during the dark hours of the Chernobyl disaster. The echoes of this narrative resound even today, resonating across time and space, carrying with them a solemn message that resonates beyond borders.

Time, a relentless healer, has quietly wrought its impact on the aftermath of Chernobyl. The majority of the malevolent agents unleashed have embarked upon a journey of decay, relinquishing their potency. Yet, amidst this fading echo, certain elements such as Caesium and Plutonium stand resolute. They persist, unyielding, steadfast in their endurance within the environmental tapestry. Their legacy, as enduring as it is ominous, reaches across epochs— stretching over hundreds, and even thousands, of years. Despite the diminishment in their presence, they remain as a lingering reminder of the calamity's enduring aftermath.

Within the chronicles of the European Parliament, the tale of Forsmark stands as a testament to vigilance. It commemorates the role Sweden played in sounding the alarm during those tumultuous days. The alert they raised, woven into the fabric of history, carried a message of shared responsibility—one that transcended national boundaries and resonated with the essence of human solidarity.

The legacy of Forsmark serves as a poignant reminder that the consequences of catastrophic events such as Chernobyl cannot be confined within temporal boundaries. They transcend generations, persisting as a collective memory that serves as a beacon of caution. The enduring impact of Caesium and Plutonium, their lingering presence etched into the environment, is a humbling reminder that our actions reverberate far beyond the immediate present.

The threads that bind Forsmark's legacy to the global narrative weave a tale of shared concern—a concern that transcends politics and borders, uniting nations under the common banner of safeguarding our planet's future. It's a tale that urges us to acknowledge the lasting repercussions of our actions, to heed the wisdom of those who came before us, and to pave a path forward that is mindful of both our present and the indelible echoes of our past.

Conclusion Three trumpets

"The First Angel Sounded" has explored the convergence of World War I and biblical prophecy, revealing the intriguing interplay between historical events and timeless spiritual insights.

Our journey through the past has shed light on how human actions and divine teachings intersect, offering a deeper understanding of the world's intricate dynamics. The patterns we've uncovered show that history and prophecy are not isolated fragments, but interconnected threads weaving a complex tapestry.

By delving into the historical context of World War I and its alignment with biblical passages, we've discovered that ancient wisdom holds relevance even in modern times. The symphony of history unfolds according to a harmonious rhythm that resonates across centuries.

"The First Angel Sounded" encourages us to contemplate the significance of past events and their relationship with prophecy. It underscores the enduring relevance of sacred texts as guides for interpreting the unfolding of human affairs. Through this exploration, we've learned that the tapestry of existence is woven with purpose, inviting us to engage in a thoughtful examination of our world's interconnected narratives.

As we bring our exploration to a close, let us carry forward the insights gained, fostering a deeper appreciation for the intricate interweaving of human actions and divine orchestrations. "The First Angel Sounded" invites us to continue seeking understanding, expanding our perspectives, and recognizing the echoes of ancient prophecies in the unfolding story of our lives.

"The Second Angel Sounded" takes us a step further and into the Second World War. This war centred around control of the High Seas and especially around the shores of the warring countries. That is why Hitler invaded France and Norway and Russia with the Blitzkrieg. That is why Britain needed the USA desperately to get their sea convoys through. That is also why Japan attacked Pearl Harbour as a pre-emptive strike to wipe out the American Pacific fleet. And that is why the Bible refers the war at sea and under the sea in the Second Trumpet! Jesus was asked this question privately by His disciples: "Tell us, when shall these things be? and what shall be the sign of thy coming, and of the end of the world?" Mathew 24:3. Jesus answered them firstly by referring to the pervasive spirit of deception that would be and then He said in verse 6: "And ye shall hear of wars and rumours of wars: see that ye be not troubled: for all these things must come to pass, but the end is not yet". Therefore, it becomes very clear that the end times or the beginning of sorrows starts off with deception and a huge war and rumours of wars and as we have seen the Great War to end all wars and its even bigger second World War fits the bill perfectly! The first trumpet equals the first World War ("The Great War") and then follows the Second World War which is proclaimed by the Second Trumpet of Revelation. This in turn is followed by the Cold War which runs into the third Trumpet which announces the Chernobyl Disaster and flows into the destruction of the old USSR and ends the Cold War! The rumours of wars is a sign of the times by itself. The rumours equal the eye of the camera and live streaming like the Ukrainian War which you can follow live through the camera lens as it happens! Never before was this possible! It could take months before the rumour of a war was heard. In verse 7 Jesus tells us nation shall rise against nation and kingdom against kingdom. He also mentions famines, pestilences, earthquakes, in different places. We have mentioned these like the Spanish Influenza during and after WW1as well as the hunger as a means of war. All part of the First Trumpet of WW1. The Great Influenza epidemic during and after affected a third of the world population and killed possibly as high as 100 million making it one of the deadliest pandemics in history. <u>Spanish flu - Wikipedia</u>

Today we know all about Covid 19 and other man - made killers.

It is worth mentioning that Jesus used the word nation against nation but when looked at it in the original Greek language it becomes ethnos.

Strongs 1484 ethnos - ἔθνος = a race, people, nation; the nations, heathen world,

Ethnic cleansing now gets a new meaning. Wars now moves toward ethnic wars. But Jesus also told us not to be troubled. If we endure to the end we will be saved. He will not forsake us any part of the way. Everything will end in the Great Tribulation but the time will be shortened.

Matthew 24:14

14 And this gospel of the kingdom shall be preached in all the world for a witness unto all nations; and then shall the end come.

We will be witnesses!

Printed in the United States
by Baker & Taylor Publisher Services